Every Day Has it's Own Beauty

Every day has it's own beauty...

Every day has it's
own beauty...

Every day has it's
own beauty...

Every day has it's
own beauty...

Every day has it's
own beauty...

Every day has it's
own beauty...

Every day has it's
own beauty...

Every day has it's
own beauty...

Every day has it's own beauty...

*Every day has it's
own beauty...*

Every day has it's
own beauty...

Every day has it's
own beauty...

Every day has it's
own beauty...

Every day has it's
own beauty...

Every day has it's
own beauty...

Every day has it's
own beauty...

Every day has it's
own beauty...

*Every day has it's
own beauty...*

Every day has it's
own beauty...

*Every day has it's
own beauty...*

Every day has it's
own beauty...

Every day has it's
own beauty...

Every day has it's
own beauty...

*Every day has it's
own beauty...*

Every day has it's
own beauty...

Every day has it's
own beauty...

Every day has it's
own beauty...

Every day has it's
own beauty...

Every day has it's
own beauty...

Every day has it's
own beauty...

Every day has it's
own beauty...

Every day has it's
own beauty...

Every day has it's
own beauty...

Every day has it's
own beauty...

Every day has it's own beauty...

Every day has it's
own beauty...

Every day has it's
own beauty...

Every day has it's
own beauty...

Every day has it's
own beauty...

Every day has it's own beauty...

Every day has it's own beauty...

*Every day has it's
own beauty...*

Every day has it's
own beauty...

Every day has it's
own beauty...

Every day has it's

own beauty...

Every day has it's
own beauty...

*Every day has it's
own beauty...*

Every day has it's
own beauty...

Every day has it's own beauty...

Every day has it's
own beauty...

*Every day has it's
own beauty...*

*Every day has it's
own beauty...*

Every day has it's
own beauty...

Every day has it's
own beauty...

Every day has it's
own beauty...

Every day has it's own beauty...

Every day has it's
own beauty...

Every day has it's
own beauty...

Every day has it's
own beauty...

Every day has it's
own beauty...

Every day has it's own beauty...

Every day has it's own beauty...

Every day has it's
own beauty...

Every day has it's
own beauty...

Every day has it's
own beauty...

Every day has it's
own beauty...

Every day has it's
own beauty...

Every day has it's own beauty...

Every day has it's
own beauty...

Every day has it's own beauty...

Every day has it's
own beauty...

Every day has it's
own beauty...

Every day has it's own beauty...

Every day has it's
own beauty...

*Every day has it's
own beauty...*

Every day has it's
own beauty...

Every day has it's
own beauty...

Every day has it's
own beauty...

Every day has it's
own beauty...

Every day has it's
own beauty...

Every day has it's
own beauty...

Every day has it's
own beauty...

Every day has it's own beauty...

Every day has it's
own beauty...

Every day has it's
own beauty...

Every day has it's
own beauty...

Every day has it's own beauty...

Every day has it's
own beauty...

Every day has it's
own beauty...

Every day has it's
own beauty...

Every day has it's
own beauty...

Every day has it's
own beauty...

Every day has it's own beauty...

*Every day has it's
own beauty...*

Every day has it's
own beauty...

*Every day has it's
own beauty...*

Every day has it's own beauty...

Every day has it's
own beauty...

Every day has it's own beauty...

Every day has it's
own beauty...

Every day has it's own beauty...

Every day has it's
own beauty...

Every day has it's
own beauty...

Every day has it's
own beauty...

Every day has it's
own beauty...

Every day has it's
own beauty...

Every day has it's own beauty...

Every day has it's
own beauty...

*Every day has it's
own beauty...*

Every day has it's
own beauty...

Every day has it's
own beauty...

Every day has it's
own beauty...

Every day has it's
own beauty...

Every day has it's
own beauty...

Every day has it's
own beauty...

Every day has it's
own beauty...

Every day has it's
own beauty...

*Every day has it's
own beauty...*

Every day has it's
own beauty...

Every day has it's
own beauty...

Every day has it's
own beauty...

Every day has it's
own beauty...

Every day has it's
own beauty...

Every day has it's
own beauty...

*Every day has it's
own beauty...*

Every day has it's
own beauty...

Every day has it's
own beauty...

Every day has it's
own beauty...

Every day has it's
own beauty...

Every day has it's
own beauty...

Every day has it's
own beauty...

Every day has it's
own beauty...

Every day has it's
own beauty...

Every day has it's
own beauty...

Every day has it's
own beauty...

Every day has it's
own beauty...

Every day has it's own beauty...

*Every day has it's
own beauty...*

Every day has it's
own beauty...

*Every day has it's
own beauty...*

Every day has it's own beauty...

Every day has it's
own beauty...

*Every day has it's
own beauty...*

Every day has it's
own beauty...

Every day has it's
own beauty...

Every day has it's
own beauty...

Every day has it's
own beauty...

Every day has it's
own beauty...

Every day has it's own beauty...

*Every day has it's
own beauty...*